We're from Pakistan

Emma Lynch

Heinemann
LIBRARY

Young Explorer

H **www.heinemann.co.uk/library**
Visit our website to find out more information about **Heinemann Library** books.

To order:
☎ Phone 44 (0) 1865 888066
▤ Send a fax to 44 (0) 1865 314091
💻 Visit the Heinemann Bookshop at www.heinemann.co.uk/library to browse our catalogue and order online.

First published in Great Britain by Heinemann Library, Halley Court, Jordan Hill, Oxford OX2 8EJ, part of Harcourt Education.
Heinemann is a registered trademark of Harcourt Education Ltd.

Editorial: Jilly Attwood and Kate Bellamy
Design: Ron Kamen and Celia Jones
Illustrations: Darreb Lingard
Photographer: Sharron Lovell
Picture Research: Maria Joannou and Erica Newbery
Production: Séverine Ribierre

Originated by Ambassador Litho Ltd
Printed and bound in China by South China Printing Company

ISBN 0 431 11950 3
09 08 07 06 05
10 9 8 7 6 5 4 3 2 1

British Library Cataloguing in Publication Data

Lynch, Emma
We're From Pakistan
954.9'1053

A full catalogue record for this book is available from the British Library.

Acknowledgements

The publishers would like to thank the following for permission to reproduce photographs: Audrius Tomonis p. **30c**; Harcourt Education pp. **1, 5a, 5b, 6a, 6b, 7a, 7b, 8a, 8b, 9a, 9b, 10, 11a, 11b, 12, 13a, 13b, 14a, 14b, 15, 16a, 16b, 17a, 17b, 18a, 18b, 19a, 19b, 20a, 20b, 21, 22a, 22b, 23a, 23b, 24, 25a, 25b, 26a, 26b, 27a, 27b, 28a, 28b, 29a, 29b, 30a, 30b** (Sharron Lovell).

Cover photograph of Shazia and her brothers, reproduced with permission of Harcourt Education/Sharron Lovell.

Our thanks to Tanvi Rai for her assistance in the preparation of this book.

Every effort has been made to contact copyright holders of any material reproduced in this book. Any omissions will be rectified in subsequent printings if notice is given to the publishers.

The paper used to print this book comes from sustainable resources.

Contents

Words appearing in the text in bold, **like this**, are explained in the Glossary.

 Find out more about Pakistan at www.heinemannexplore.co.uk

Where is Pakistan?

To learn more about Pakistan we meet three children who live there. Pakistan is a country in Asia. It is near India and China.

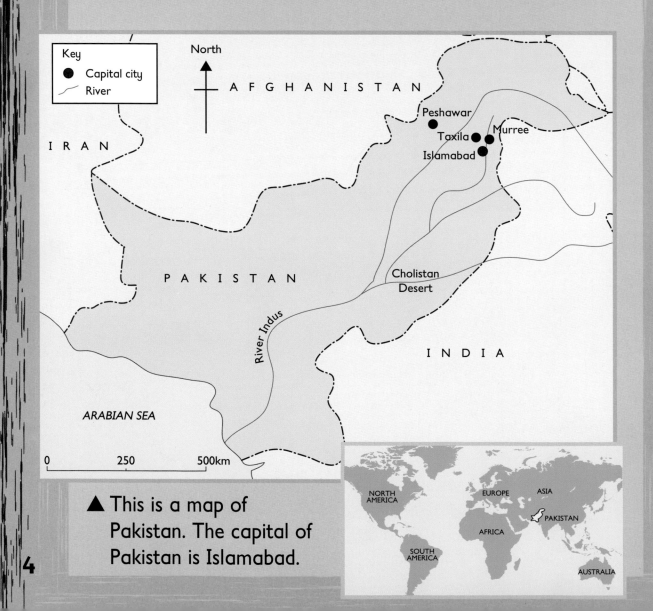

Key
● Capital city
⌇ River

North

AFGHANISTAN

IRAN

Peshawar
Taxila
Murree
Islamabad

PAKISTAN

Cholistan
Desert

River Indus

INDIA

ARABIAN SEA

0   250   500km

NORTH AMERICA
EUROPE
ASIA
PAKISTAN
AFRICA
SOUTH AMERICA
AUSTRALIA

▲ This is a map of Pakistan. The capital of Pakistan is Islamabad.

The weather in Pakistan is mostly hot, but it can be cold in the north. Sometimes there are **earthquakes** in Pakistan. At certain times of the year there are also **monsoons**.

▼ There are busy towns in Pakistan.

▼ Most people in Pakistan live in the countryside.

Meet Kynat

Kynat is eight years old. She lives in Islamabad, the capital city of Pakistan. Kynat lives with her mother, father and older sister.

Kynat's father

Kynat's mother

Kynat

Kynat's sister

Kynat's mother makes ▶
chapattis for the family.

In the evening, the family eat
a meal together. Kynat's
mother cooks the food. The
family likes to eat rice,
chapattis and curry.

Kynat's school

Kynat goes to school six days a week. She learns maths, English, **Urdu** and art. Kynat likes English but she does not like maths.

▲ There are 50 children in Kynat's class.

Kynat's class practise cricket and hockey in the school yard. At playtime, Kynat plays clapping and skipping games with her friends.

◄ Kynat and her sister play skipping games at home too.

Having fun

When Kynat is not at school, she likes flying her kite. The roof of Kynat's house is flat. Kynat and her sister can play on the roof. Kynat flies her kite there.

◀ For festivals Kynat has **henna** painted on her hands.

Kynat wears a long shirt and loose trousers. This is called a *shalwar kameez*. For **festivals**, like **Eid**, she wears a special *shalwar kameez*.

Festivals

There are many **festivals** in Pakistan. People and animals wear special clothes at festival time. They eat food sold at stalls on the street. Sometimes they dance too.

kite

Every year there is a kite festival in Pakistan. On kite day, lots of people fly their kites. There are hundreds of kites in the sky!

Meet Omar

Omar is seven years old. He lives in a city called Peshawar. Omar lives with his mother, father, younger brother, grandparents, three uncles and two aunts.

▼ Omar has a large family.

Omar's father

Omar's grandparents

Omar's mother

Omar's brother

Omar

Omar's father makes new clothes for people. He is a **tailor**. His mother works at home. Omar would like to be a doctor when he grows up.

Omar's father is very busy ▶ making new clothes before the **festival** of **Eid**.

At home

Omar likes to help his mother. He looks after his younger brother, Mosseen, while his mother does her work. He likes playing games with Mosseen.

Omar's favourite food is black-eyed beans and naan bread. His family buy food at the fair when it comes to town. Omar likes to drink the fresh fruit juice that is made at the fair.

Omar's day

Omar goes to school in the mornings. He has to wear a school uniform. In the afternoon, Omar goes to a class to study the **Qur'an** for an hour.

Omar and his best friend, ▶ Muzammin, are learning to read the Qur'an.

Omar likes looking after his pet birds.
He is also learning to play cricket.
Sometimes he watches cartoons with
his brother.

◀ Omar keeps his
pet birds on the
roof of his house.

Travelling in Pakistan

In the towns people travel in cars. They also travel in large buses. It is cheap to travel in **rickshaws** and in horse-drawn cars.

The buses in Pakistan ▶ can be very colourful.

In the country, there are not many buses or cars so people have to walk. People often walk a long way. Sometimes they carry things on their head as they walk. They also ride on camels.

This girl finds it easier to ▶ hold the heavy pot on her head than in her arms.

Meet Shazia

Shazia is eight years old. She lives in a small village called Cholistan. Shazia lives with her mother, father, brothers, sister, uncle and aunt.

Shazia's mother

Shazia's aunt

Shazia's sister

Shazia's uncle

Shazia

Shazia's father

Shazia's brothers

Cholistan is in ▶ the **desert**.

Shazia's parents are farmers. ▶
They own a small shop too.

Shazia's house is made of
mud, wood and straw. They
have no water or electricity
in the house. There is lots
of land around the house
where Shazia can play.

23

Life in cholistan

Shazia and her family look forward to two special **festivals**. One is **Eid** and the other is a spring festival. When there is a festival, Shazia wears a new *shalwar kameez*.

▼ Shazia is learning to sew, so she can make her own *shalwar kameez*.

Cholistan is the hottest, driest part of Pakistan. In the summer there is very little water. Shazia's family have to get water from a deep well. They also have a camel.

▲ Shazia's family have a camel. Camels can store water so they do not get thirsty very often.

School and work

Shazia's school only has one class. Shazia and her brothers and sister are all taught together. They have their lessons outside. Lessons are taught in **Urdu**.

Shazia walks to school with her father and brother. ▶

After school, Shazia sometimes helps in her parents' shop. She also feeds the farm animals, and helps her mother with the cooking.

▲ The goats are Shazia's favourite animals.

Places to visit

2000 years ago, many people travelled across Pakistan buying and selling silk. The road they travelled on became famous. It was called the Silk Road. Taxila was a city on the Silk Road.

▼ Today, people visit the old buildings at Taxila.

◀ Silk and sewing are still important in Pakistan.

cable car

There is a good view of Murree from the cable car. ▶

Murree is a city in the hills. People visit it in the summer because it is cooler than other parts of Pakistan. They travel up the hill by **cable car**.

Pakistani fact file

Flag   **Capital city**   **Money**

Islamabad   Rupee

Religion
• Around 97 percent of people in Pakistan are Muslims.

Language
• **Urdu** is the official language of Pakistan, but people also speak Punjabi, Sindhi, Siraiki, Pashtu and English.

Try speaking Urdu!
Subah bakhair .... Good morning.
Kaysay ho? .... How are you?
Bohatt shukria .... Thanks a lot.

 Find out more about Pakistan at
www.heinemannexplore.co.uk

Glossary

cable car car that moves along an overhead cable to take people up and down mountains

chapatti thin, flat bread

desert very hot, dry area of land that has almost no rain and very few plants

earthquake sudden movement of the ground caused by rocks under the earth

Eid Eid means celebration and is a very important time for Muslims. Eid-Al-Fitr is at the end of Ramadan, the month of fasting.

festival big celebration for a town or country

henna reddish dye that comes from the leaves of the henna plant

monsoon season of heavy rain

Qur'an Muslim holy book

rickshaw two wheeled cart with a hood, pulled by one or two people

tailor someone who makes clothes

Urdu official language of Pakistan

More books to read

Fiesta: Pakistan, I Dore, (Franklin Watts, 2001)

Country Insights: Pakistan, Eaniqa Khan and Rob Unwin, (Hodder Wayland, 2000)

Index

Titles in the *We're from...* series include:

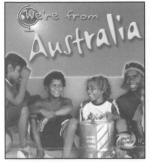

Hardback   0 431 11935 X

Hardback   0 431 11951 1

Hardback   0 431 11946 5

Hardback   0 431 11932 5

Hardback   0 431 11937 6

Hardback   0 431 11933 3

Hardback   0 431 11947 3

Hardback   0 431 11949 X

Hardback   0 431 11936 8

Hardback   0 431 11948 1

Hardback   0 431 11934 1

Hardback   0 431 11950 3

Find out about the other titles in this series on our website www.heinemann.co.uk/library

914.11

Countries Around the World

Scotland

Melanie Waldron

www.raintreepublishers.co.uk
Visit our website to find out
more information about
Raintree books.

To order:

☎ Phone 0845 6044371

🖹 Fax +44 (0) 1865 312263

🖳 Email myorders@raintreepublishers.co.uk

Customers from outside the UK please telephone +44 1865 312262

Raintree is an imprint of **Capstone Global Library Limited**, a
company incorporated in England and Wales having its registered
office at 7 Pilgrim Street, London, EC4V 6LB – Registered company
number: 6695582

Text © Capstone Global Library Limited 2012
First published in hardback in 2012
The moral rights of the proprietor have been asserted.

Edited by Louise Galpine, Kate DeVilliers, and Laura Knowles
Designed by Richard Parker
Original illustrations © Capstone Global Library Ltd 2011
Illustrated by Oxford Designers & Illustrators
Picture research by Liz Alexander
Originated by Capstone Global Library Ltd
Printed in China by CTPS

ISBN 978 1 4062 2803 8
15 14 13 12 11
10 9 8 7 6 5 4 3 2 1

British Library Cataloguing in Publication Data
Waldron, Melanie.
Scotland. -- (Countries around the world)
941.1'086-dc22
A full catalogue record for this book is available from the
British Library.

Acknowledgments
We would like to thank the following for permission to reproduce
photographs: Alamy pp. **13** (© Banana Pancake), **17** (© Wig
Worland), **19** (© Roger Covey), **23** (© david tipling), **26** (© tom
Kidd); © AWS Ocean Energy Ltd p. **36**; Corbis pp. **5** (© Ocean),
11 (© David Moir/Reuters); iStockphoto p. **25** (© Chris Hepburn);
Photolibrary pp. **22** (John Tomkins), **29** (epa), **33** (Paul Harris);
Press Association Images p. **32** (Lynne Cameron/PA Archive);
Shutterstock pp. **9** (© TTphoto), **15** (© Yvan), **18** (© John A
Cameron), **21** (© Sue Robinson), **20** (© Ian McDonald), **31**
(© Morag Fleming), **35** (© Robert Anthony), **34** (© Paul Cowan),
46 (© Gary Blakeley), **37** (© Aga & Tomek Adameczek).

Cover photograph of a street entertainer walking the tightrope
at the Edinburgh festival reproduced with permission of Alamy/
© John McKenna.

We would like to thank Rob Bowden for his invaluable help in the
preparation of this book.

Every effort has been made to contact copyright holders of material
reproduced in this book. Any omissions will be rectified in
subsequent printings if notice is given to the publisher.

Disclaimer
All the Internet addresses (URLs) given in this book were valid at
the time of going to press. However, due to the dynamic nature of
the Internet, some addresses may have changed, or sites may have
changed or ceased to exist since publication. While the author
and publisher regret any inconvenience this may cause readers, no
responsibility for any such changes can be accepted by either the
author or the publisher.

Contents

Some words are printed in bold, **like this**. You can find out what they mean by looking in the glossary.

Introducing Scotland

What comes into your mind when you think of Scotland? Do you think of mountains and misty moors, **bagpipes** and **haggis**? Or do you think of beautiful, vibrant cities and a modern mix of people? Well, both images are correct. Scotland is a unique country with a strong sense of belonging.

Scotland is one of the four countries, along with England, Wales, and Northern Ireland, that make up the United Kingdom (UK). Scotland is the northernmost country of the UK, located in the northwest corner of Europe. However, Scotland has not always been part of the UK. For many centuries Scotland was an independent nation, with an uneasy relationship with England.

The land and the people

Large parts of Scotland are wilderness, with huge mountain ranges and moorlands creating a wonderful sense of space. The islands along the western coast add to the beauty of the landscape. Here you can find beautiful white sandy beaches alongside stark mountain cliffs.

The varying landscape and the history of Scotland have created a lasting and distinct **culture**. Scottish people are very proud of their country and have a strong sense of Scottishness. However, Scots are also keen to welcome new cultures into Scotland, to move forward together in the 21st century.

How to say...

Most Scottish people speak English. The ancient language of Gaelic is spoken by fewer than 2 per cent of the population. It is common only in the northwest. Scots is another ancient language, and today many Scottish people still use some Scots words.

| **Gaelic:** | Scotland | *Alba* | **Scots:** | mountain | *ben* |
| | mountain | *beinn* | | beautiful | *bonny* |

Eilean Donan Castle has been described as the most beautiful castle in Scotland. It sits on the northwest coast where three lochs (lakes) join, and looks outwards towards the island of Skye.

History: a people united

Before Scotland came together as a nation, **Celtic tribes** called Picts lived on the land. At this time Scotland was known as Caledonia. The Picts kept the Romans out so Caledonia never became part of the Roman Empire.

The Scotti invade

In the 6th century, Irish Celts called Scotti started invading the west coast of Caledonia. The Scotti and the Picts were united under Kenneth MacAlpin in AD 843. However it was not until King Malcolm II defeated the **Anglo-Saxons** in the south, around 1018, that Scotland was born.

Invaders!

In the 8th century, Vikings began to invade from the north. They killed villagers before taking anything of value. The Vikings took control of some areas, before finally giving all the land back between 1232 and 1469.

The Wars of Independence

King Edward I of England invaded Scotland in 1296. This angered the Scots, who came together to resist him. The English were defeated in 1297 at Stirling Bridge. The fighting carried on for over 300 years. One famous battle was in 1314, when Robert the Bruce led the Scots to victory at Bannockburn.

SIR WILLIAM WALLACE (c.1270-1305)

Wallace was a strong leader who united the Scots against Edward I. His army killed 5,000 English troops at Stirling Bridge. Wallace was eventually captured and brutally killed by the English in 1305. The Wallace Monument near Stirling was built to remember him.

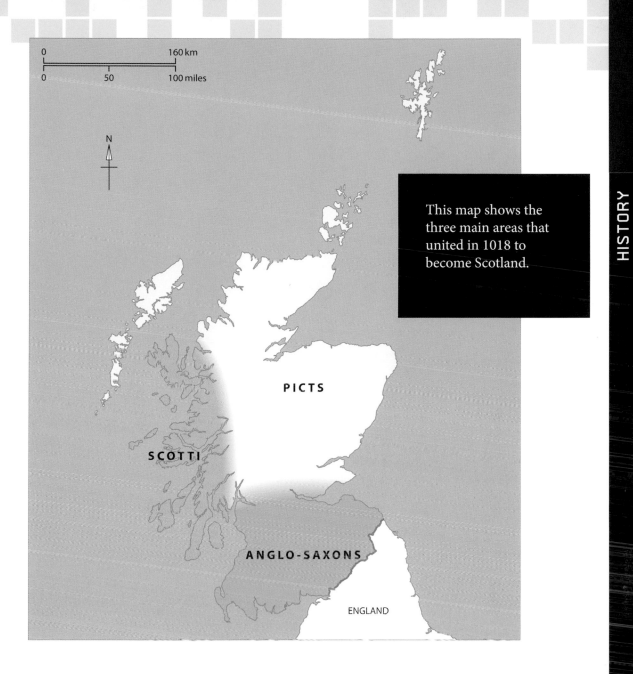

This map shows the three main areas that united in 1018 to become Scotland.

PICTS

SCOTTI

ANGLO-SAXONS

ENGLAND

Risings and revolution

From 1603 Scotland and England were ruled by one king or queen, although the two countries were separate. By the end of the 17th century, civil war had ruined Scotland's **economy** and people were dying from **famine**. Scotland's powerful **nobles** knew joining with England was the only solution. In 1707 the Treaty of Union was signed and the United Kingdom was born.

Jacobite risings

Many **Highland** Scots wanted the **Catholic** descendants of James I to rule again, instead of the **Protestant** monarchy (king or queen) that was in place in the 1700s. These rebels, called Jacobites, included Charles Edward Stuart. He was also known as "Bonnie Prince Charlie". With his army, he marched as far south as Derby in England. However, he retreated and was finally defeated at the Battle of Culloden in 1746.

The Highland Clearances

During the late 18th and early 19th centuries, landowners in the north and west realized that sheep farming would bring them a lot of money. So they began to force **tenants** to leave their land, making up to 100,000 people homeless. Some went to live by the coast, to make a living from the sea. Others fled to cities in search of work. Thousands **emigrated** to places such as Canada, the United States, Australia, and New Zealand.

The Industrial Revolution

While the Clearances were a dark time in the Highlands, the Scottish Lowlands were flourishing. During the **Industrial Revolution**, Scotland became a leading **industrialized** country. Steam power led to big advances in **manufacturing**. Large-scale railway-building meant that goods could travel long distances. Glasgow became a world centre for shipbuilding. Many people flocked to the cities to find work, so while the Highlands were losing people, the cities were growing rapidly.

Daily life

In the late 18th and early 19th centuries, most of the people who moved to Glasgow ended up living in tenements (blocks of flats). For the poorest people, these flats were often squalid and very cramped. Many had only one or two rooms housing entire families. Nearly half of all children died before reaching their fifth birthday.

The Forth Rail Bridge was finally completed in 1890. It is over 2.5 kilometres (1.5 miles) long. Up to 4,000 men worked on the bridge, and 57 men were killed during its construction.

Into the 21st century

Events in the 20th century left many Scots keen to break away from the UK government. Some economic **policies** were crippling Scotland, while at the same time allowing businesses in England to prosper. Money from North Sea oil, found in Scottish areas of the sea, was not benefiting most Scots. Many people wanted change.

In September 1997, Scots **voted** for the creation of a Scottish **parliament**. Elections to the parliament took place in May 1999 and it was officially opened by Queen Elizabeth II in July 1999.

Modern Scotland

Since the Scottish parliament was set up in 1999, Scotland has looked to the future with new confidence and pride. Having lost large numbers of people through emigration, Scots are very welcoming to anyone wishing to live and work in Scotland. Many Irish **immigrants** arrived in the 19th century, followed by Italians in the early 20th century. Immigrants from Bangladesh, India, and Pakistan arrived in the late 20th century. Today's immigrants come mainly from eastern Europe. Most Scots, of all backgrounds, feel a very strong loyalty to their local city, town, or region. However, as a whole the people of modern Scotland stand together to take their place in the UK, Europe, and the rest of the world.

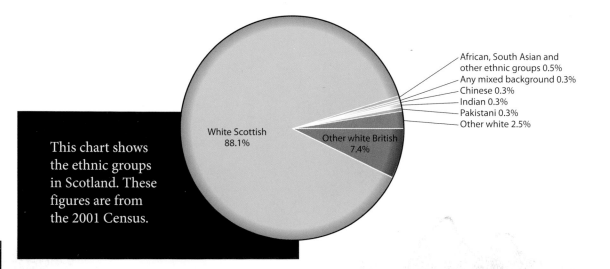

African, South Asian and other ethnic groups 0.5%
Any mixed background 0.3%
Chinese 0.3%
Indian 0.3%
Pakistani 0.3%
Other white 2.5%

White Scottish 88.1%

Other white British 7.4%

This chart shows the ethnic groups in Scotland. These figures are from the 2001 Census.

YOUNG PEOPLE

A truly 21st century sport has come to Scotland! The sport of *parkour*, or "free-running", originally came from France. It involves crossing urban landscapes by vaulting, leaping, and climbing over obstacles. There are growing groups in Aberdeen, Edinburgh, and Glasgow, who meet in the cities to train together and practise some really tricky moves!

The T in the Park music festival is an example of Scotland's new modern and vibrant outlook.

Regions and resources: land, industry, and technology

What is Scotland like? The natural landscape dominates a lot of Scotland, while the **urban** and industrial areas continue to change and grow.

The Highlands and islands

Much of the north and west of Scotland is a mix of mountain and **moorland**. The Grampian Mountains are huge, rounded mountains in the middle of Scotland. These mountains are separated from the northern Highlands by the Great Glen. This is a long line of deep connected lochs (lakes). It is a huge **fault** in the Earth's crust. North and west of the Great Glen, more mountains give way to hundreds of islands.

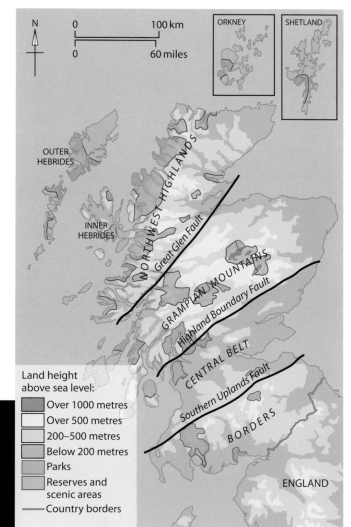

This map shows the **topography** of Scotland and some of the parks and reserves that help to preserve the landscape.

Land height above sea level:
- Over 1000 metres
- Over 500 metres
- 200–500 metres
- Below 200 metres
- Parks
- Reserves and scenic areas
- Country borders

The Great Glen is a spectacular and ancient feature of the Scottish landscape.

The Central Belt and Lowlands

The Central Belt lies south of the Highland Boundary Fault, which separates the Highlands from the Lowlands. This region is densely populated and includes Glasgow and Edinburgh, Scotland's largest cities. Most of Scotland's farming and industry is located here.

The Borders and Dumfries & Galloway lie south of the Southern Upland Fault. As the name suggests, the Borders region forms part of the border with England. It is a hilly region with market towns dotted across the landscape.

Daily life

School pupils living on the tiny island of Papa Westray in northern Scotland usually catch a ferry every day. This takes them to school on the neighbouring island of Westray. However, for a few months in 2009 their ferry could not make the journey. The solution? The children travelled to school on the world's shortest flight! The flight, about 1.6 kilometres (1 mile), takes just over one minute!

Scotland's 21st century economy

Many old, heavy industries in Scotland have now been replaced by new ideas, new business, and new jobs. The government is now promoting certain industries. After the global economic problems that began in 2008, Scotland's **unemployment** rate rose slightly to around eight per cent. Investment in the following growing industries will give Scotland and its population good reason to feel positive about the future:

- **Life sciences:** Life sciences include biotechnology, which is using living things to improve human health and the environment.

- **Finance and services:** This includes the many call-centres in Scotland. Apparently people trust a Scottish accent!

- **Computing and electronics:** This growing industry gave rise to the name "Silicon Glen", an area in the Central Belt where many businesses have set up.

- **Energy:** There is a large focus on developing new technologies for **renewable energy.**

- **Creative industries:** This exciting area includes fashion, design, advertising, film, performing arts, publishing, and music.

- **Tourism and outdoor pursuits:** This will build upon Scotland's existing reputation as an excellent tourist destination.

- **Universities:** Cutting-edge university research is attracting many students and **investors** into Scotland.

DOLLY THE SHEEP

Dolly the sheep, born in July 1996, was the first living mammal to be **cloned**. She was created at a biotechnology research institute near Edinburgh. She had four lambs. Dolly died in 2003 and her remains are on show at the Royal Museum of Scotland in Edinburgh.

These cyclists are competing in the 2008 Mountain Bike World Cup, at the Nevis Range near Fort William.

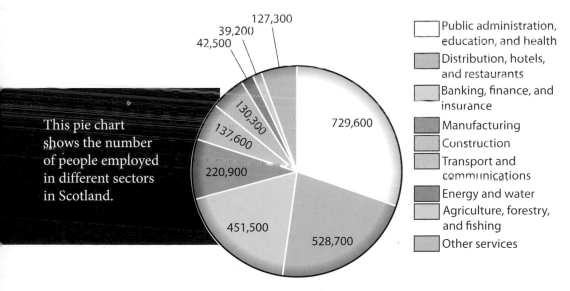

This pie chart shows the number of people employed in different sectors in Scotland.

127,300
39,200
42,500
130,300
137,600
220,900
451,500
729,600
528,700

- Public administration, education, and health
- Distribution, hotels, and restaurants
- Banking, finance, and insurance
- Manufacturing
- Construction
- Transport and communications
- Energy and water
- Agriculture, forestry, and fishing
- Other services

Wildlife: a precious resource

Is Scotland's environment a precious resource? At first glance, large areas seem to be fairly empty of life. But look a bit closer . . .

The disappearing forest

Up until about 2,000 years ago, most of Scotland was forested with beech, oak, ash, rowan, birch, and pine. Today only small pockets of this **primeval** forest remain. Large areas were cleared for fuel, timber, and grazing, leaving behind the **heathland** that we see today.

Much of the heathland is covered in heather, which produces a carpet of pink and purple flowers in late summer. In May yellow gorse flowers take their turn. Many insect-eating plants live in damp areas like **peat boglands**. Alpine plants and rare mosses and lichens grow well in the high, rocky mountainous areas.

Pink and purple heather flowers make a beautiful carpet over the mountains.

Thickly planted forests harm wildlife, destroying their natural habitat.

New forests

Huge **plantations** of conifers were created on poor land from the 1950s onwards, to provide softwood timber. The problem with these forests is that very little light reaches the forest floor, so no plants can grow underneath, and very few animals can live there. However, all new plantations must now be managed so that a more diverse range of plants and animals can flourish there.

How to say...

Gaelic:	forest	*coille*
	heather	*fraoch*
Scots:	stone	*stane*
	lake	*loch*
	valley	*glen*
	cold, wet weather	*dreich*
	stream	*burn*
	hill	*brae*

A haven for wildlife

Scotland's vast areas of uninhabited land have provided a home for many different animals for hundreds of years. However, some **species**, for example wolves and wild boar, have been hunted to **extinction**. Today the threats to wildlife are habitat change, for example bogs being drained for farmland. But there is still much to see, with some patience and a bit of knowledge!

Red deer are the largest type of deer found in the United Kingdom.

Huge herds of deer roam the Highlands and moorlands. Pine martens and **endangered**, secretive wildcats live in forested areas. Sleek otters play around the coastline and red squirrels thrive in the Highlands. Bird spotters will find capercaillie, ptarmigan, golden eagles, and the rare and endangered corncrake.

Cows, sheep, and ponies

Scotland also has some native domestic animals, which are a bit easier to find! Soay sheep, originally from the island of St Kilda, have soft brown wool. Aberdeen Angus cattle have beautiful black coats and are raised for beef. Highland cattle are a favourite symbol of Scotland, with their shaggy brown coats and long horns. The tiny Shetland ponies and slightly larger Eriskay ponies are hardy enough to survive harsh Scottish winters outside.

Should wolves be reintroduced?

Wolves became extinct in Scotland in the 18th century. Many people are now campaigning for them to be reintroduced. This would help to keep deer numbers down, and so delicate **ecosystems** damaged by large deer herds would recover. However, opponents fear that wolves would also prey on farm animals, and estate owners would lose money as there would be less **deer stalking**. What do you think?

This is a Scottish wildcat. Wildcats are much bigger than house cats.

The coast and the sea

Scotland's coast is dotted with around 790 islands. Most are found off the north and west coasts. There are three main groups:

- Northern Isles – includes Shetland and Orkney
- Outer Hebrides – includes Lewis and Harris
- Inner Hebrides – includes Skye, Mull, and Iona.

Most of the islands are **uninhabited**. Many have glorious white sandy beaches, while others have steep sea cliffs. The coast of the Outer Hebrides is dominated by machair. This is one of the rarest habitats in Europe. Machair is made from shell sand. Beautiful wildflowers such as wild thyme thrive there. The pristine environment attracts many tourists. A fine balance must be kept so the tourists don't harm the very habitat they have come to see. Some areas are also being affected by **erosion**.

These volunteers are helping to clear rubbish from a beach in southwest Scotland.

Beautiful wildflowers grow on machair at Balranald reserve in the Outer Hebrides.

Bird life and sea life

Many internationally important **migrating** birds visit Scotland's coastal areas. Puffins, skuas, gannets, guillemots, fulmars, and shearwaters are among the visitors. The seas are also full of life. Bottlenose dolphins, orcas, humpback whales, common and grey seals, and porpoises are commonly seen around the coast.

In recent years, some sea life has been affected by pollution from salmon fish farms. These provide an important source of salmon, as wild salmon is becoming endangered. However, many fish farms are now trying to reduce their impact. The biggest threat to sea life comes from rubbish. Hundreds of animals die every year after mistaking plastic bags for food and eating them.

It is clear that Scotland's wildlife and environment are unique and very precious.

Infrastructure: Scotland's systems

The Scottish Parliament was established in 1999. It can make policies in certain areas. These include:

- agriculture
- education
- environment
- forestry and fishing
- health
- sport and the arts
- tourism and economic development.

Other policies, for example in defence, foreign policy, and social security can only be dealt with by the UK Parliament. There are 129 Members of the Scottish Parliament (MSPs) and they are elected by the Scottish people every four years. Thirty-five per cent of them are women. The Scottish Government is made up of members of the winning political party. In 2010, the Scottish National Party (SNP) formed the government, with Alex Salmond at the head as First Minister and Nicola Sturgeon as his deputy.

A healthy nation?

Healthcare in Scotland is provided by NHS Scotland. It is free and available to everyone. The total running cost is around £11.3 billion (2010), and it is paid for by the **taxes** that people pay. Around half the cost is spent running Scotland's hospitals.

Compared to the rest of the UK, the health of the Scottish people has been poor over the last few decades. This has been due to high levels of smoking and drinking alcohol, and to an unhealthy diet. However, Scotland's health agencies are working hard to improve the nation's health.

This is the debating chamber inside the Scottish Parliament building.

Scottish health statistics		
Life expectancy	75 (men)	80 (women)
Obesity rate	25% (men)	26% (women)
New cases of cancer per year	26,000	
Deaths from cancer per year	15,000	

A literate country

Scotland has been very proud of its education system since the 16th century. This is when the Scottish Church decided to spread education across the whole country. Scotland has many top universities that attract students from all over the world.

Children go to primary school from the age of five. When they are twelve, they go to secondary school. They must remain at school until they are at least 16. Most schools have a uniform, with a summer version and a winter version. The school day usually starts around 9 a.m. and ends around 3 p.m. for primary schools and 4 p.m. for secondary schools.

Daily life

Some of the primary schools on Scotland's islands, for example Canna, are tiny. There is only one classroom, and often only one teacher who is also the headteacher.

At the school on the tiny island of Canna there are only two pupils and one teacher!

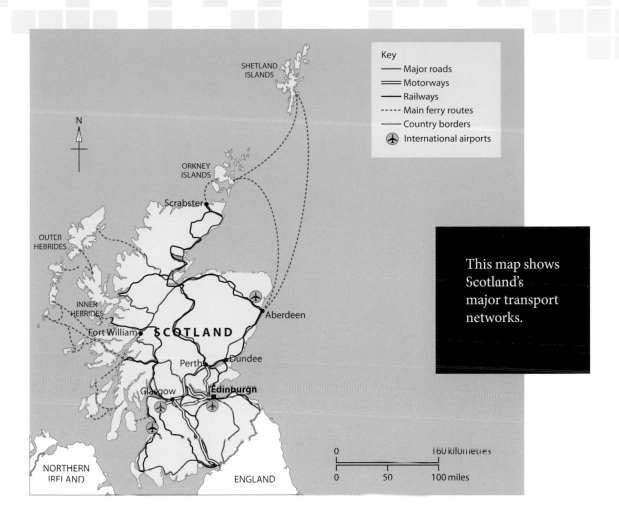

Key
— Major roads
═══ Motorways
— Railways
---- Main ferry routes
— Country borders
✈ International airports

SHETLAND
ISLANDS

N

ORKNEY
ISLANDS

Scrabster

OUTER
HEBRIDES

INNER
HEBRIDES

Fort William

SCOTLAND

Aberdeen

Perth Dundee

Glasgow Edinburgh

NORTHERN
IRELAND

ENGLAND

This map shows
Scotland's
major transport
networks.

0   160 kilometres

0   50   100 miles

Road, rail, air, and sea travel

Scotland has a good road network, with some motorways. One runs right
through Glasgow! The road network is much simpler in the Highland and
islands. This is because the lower population means fewer car journeys, and
because there are many mountains and lochs in the way. Scotland has a
well-developed railway network. Glasgow also has a subway (underground
train) and a new tram network will run in Edinburgh from 2012.

Transport to and from the islands of Scotland is mainly by ferry. Sometimes
the weather means people are stranded for a day or two. Some islands are
linked by air travel using ten small airports. At Barra airport, the runway is the
beach. There are also four international airports linking Scotland with the rest
of the UK, Europe, and the world.

Culture: the flavour of Scotland

Music in Scotland is very diverse. Traditional **ballads** and songs are still sung. Dances known as jigs and reels set the toes tapping, and bagpipes are the iconic Scottish sound. Many internationally famous bands and singers are Scottish. These include Texas, Travis, Franz Ferdinand, KT Tunstall, Amy Macdonald, and Paulo Nutini.

YOUNG PEOPLE

Many people today think a *ceilidh* is a night of traditional Scottish country dancing. While this is true, more traditional *ceilidhs* include singing, poetry, and music. Everyone is welcome to take the floor!

Words and pictures

Robert Burns is perhaps Scotland's most famous writer. His poems and songs are legendary – one of the most famous is called "Address to a Haggis"! Other writers include Sir Walter Scott, Robert Louis Stevenson, and Muriel Spark. Spark's best-known book is *The Prime of Miss Jean Brodie*. Modern writers include Ian Rankin and Irvine Welsh. The current British **poet laureate** is Carol Ann Duffy, who was born in Glasgow.

Charles Rennie Mackintosh was an artist, designer, and architect. He liked simple lines and floral motifs, and his style has inspired designs for buildings, furniture, jewellery, and art.

How to say...

Gaelic:	music	ceòl
	reel (a type of dance)	righil
Scots:	child	bairn
	drink of whisky	dram
	small	wee
	to chat	blether
	careful	canny
	grumpy	crabbit
	dripping wet	drookit

JACK VETTRIANO (BORN 1951)

One of Scotland and the UK's most popular artists is Jack Vettriano. He was born in Fife, and used to be a mining engineer. His most famous painting, *The Singing Butler*, is the most popular art print in the UK. The painting sold for £744,800 at auction in 2004.

Vettriano's *The Singing Butler* is perhaps the most popular painting in the UK.

A world-class city

Edinburgh is the capital city of Scotland. It is a beautiful, historic city, with a vibrant feel. Fashionable bars and restaurants and modern offices nestle between ancient buildings, monuments, and churches. The centre is dominated by the wonderful Edinburgh Castle.

New Year's Eve (called Hogmanay in Scotland) is an event celebrated far more in Scotland than in the rest of the UK, and perhaps the world! Edinburgh hosts one of the world's best street parties for Hogmanay, with an amazing fireworks display set around the castle.

YOUNG PEOPLE

The Edinburgh Festival and Fringe has grown since 1947 into the greatest cultural festival in the world. Acts include mime, street theatre, classical music, comedy, poetry, drama, ballet, opera, and film. The Military Tattoo is held during Festival time. It is a series of displays by military bands and teams, and is set in the castle's **esplanade**.

Gaelic in Glasgow

An Lòchran is an organization set up to promote Gaelic arts and culture in Glasgow. Gaelic is a **Celtic** language spoken mostly in the Highlands and islands. However, less than two per cent of the Scottish population now speak Gaelic, and most of these people speak English first. The Scottish Government is trying to stop Gaelic dying out completely. *An Lòchran* is helping to do that by increasing awareness of the language.

BBC Alba was launched in 2008 to provide Gaelic radio and TV programmes. It has been a big success and is certainly helping to keep Gaelic alive. *Alba* is the Gaelic word for Scotland.

Bagpipes are played and fireworks are set off over Edinburgh Castle at the finale of the Military Tattoo.

Sport and leisure

Football and rugby are the most-watched sports in Scotland. Glasgow-based football teams Rangers and Celtic are infamous for their deep rivalry. Fans have been known to fight and taunt each other with songs, flags, and chants.

Popular participation sports are walking, swimming, football, cycling, and **curling**. Golf is popular and Scotland is known throughout the world as "the home of golf". Scotland has excellent facilities for white water activities, mountain and road biking, diving, fishing, rock climbing, walking, and mountaineering. In the sport of "Munro Bagging" walkers attempt to climb all of Scotland's 283 Munros, the mountains over 914 metres (3,000 feet). Another unique Scottish sport is shinty. It is a bit like hockey but the ball can be airborne and players can tackle each other!

ISLAM FERUZ
(BORN 1995)

Islam and his family fled Somalia when he was seven, and now live in Scotland. In 2009 he was selected for the Scotland under-17 football squad. "Since my family and I came to Scotland seven years ago, we have been made to feel very welcome," he said. "It's a great country which is now my home and I will be very proud to wear the Scotland jersey."

This climber is ice-climbing up a cliff on Aonoch Moor. Scotland's landscape and winter weather are perfect for this sport!

A sporting anthem

Scotland has no official national anthem but "Flower of Scotland" has been adopted as the unofficial one. It is sung at many big sporting events. The song is about the Battle of Bannockburn in 1314, when the Scottish army defeated Edward II of England:

O Flower of Scotland
When will we see your like again
That fought and died for
Your wee bit hill and glen.
And stood against him,
Proud Edward's army,
And sent him homeward
Tae think again.

Food and drink

In past years Scotland has developed a reputation for unhealthy food, including deep-fried pizzas! However, modern Scottish cuisine is changing. There is some superb home-produce available, including lamb, beef, and game (such as deer). The seafood and fish is delicious.

A national dish

Haggis is a Scottish icon. It is made of sheep heart, liver, and lungs, minced with onion, oatmeal, **suet**, spices, and salt. Cranachan is a delicious dessert. It is made with cream, honey, whisky, raspberries, and oatmeal.

Haggis is traditionally served with mashed neeps (swede) and tatties (potatoes).

Shortbread

Ask an adult to help you make this delicious biscuit.

Ingredients

- 125 grams butter
- 55 grams caster sugar
- 180 grams plain flour

What to do

1. Preheat oven to 190° Celsius/375° Fahrenheit.
2. Beat the butter and sugar together until smooth.
3. Stir in the flour to make a smooth paste.
   Turn on to a flat surface and gently roll out
   until the paste is 1centimetre (½ inch) thick.
4. Cut into rounds or fingers and place
   onto a baking tray. Chill in the
   fridge for 20 minutes.
5. Bake in the oven for
   15–20 minutes, or until
   pale golden-brown.
   Cool on a wire rack.

A national drink

Whisky is another Scottish icon. It is a very alcoholic drink made from a type of grain called barley. The rarest bottles can fetch tens of thousands of pounds.

Irn Bru is a bright orange fruit-flavoured fizzy drink which is Scotland's second national drink! It was invented in 1901 and is known for its controversial adverts.

Scotland today

Scotland is a small country with a big reputation. Its history and its icons conjure up a wild, romantic land. It is also a thoroughly modern country whose people have much to be proud of.

A sense of . . . ?

Anyone visiting Scotland will feel the sense of pride in most Scots. The new Scottish parliament has breathed new life into the country. Scots at last feel that their country is important, valued, and a cool place to live. The culture is strong and the landscape is unique. The people are supported by excellent healthcare and education.

There is also a fabulous sense of humour in most Scots, although sometimes it is not obvious! Scots have a great ability to laugh at themselves, and make jokes about their own thriftiness (being particularly careful about money)!

Scottish energy companies are testing new ways to produce energy without harming the environment. This device on Loch Ness turns wave energy into electricity.

Tourists visit Scotland's capital city, Edinburgh, to experience its beauty, history, and culture.

The 21st century

Scotland is looking forward. New technologies, especially in the energy sector, are leading the world. New people are moving to live and work there. In remote places, the Internet is encouraging people to stay and to set up new online businesses. This is all bringing money and jobs to areas that were once very poor.

Scotland's modern cities are exciting and dynamic. At the same time, they are close enough to mountains, moorland, and the coast to allow people to escape town life. This is perhaps Scotland's biggest appeal – it can offer something for everyone.

Fact file

Official language:	English, two per cent also speak Gaelic
Capital city:	Edinburgh
Bordering country:	England
Population:	5.2 million
Birth rate:	10.7 per 1,000 population
Death rate:	11.0 per 1,000 population
Religion:	Presbyterian Kirk (Church) of Scotland: 42%; Roman Catholic: 16%; Other Christian: 7%; No religion: 28%; Other religions, the largest of which is Islam: 2%; religion not stated: 5%
National symbols:	The **thistle** is the national flower. It appears on Scottish bank notes. **Tartan** is a popular symbol of Scotland. It comes in many different designs but the basic pattern is a woven lattice with horizontal and vertical stripes of colour.
Flag:	The Saltire, or St Andrew's Cross. The flag has a blue background with a white diagonal cross. It represents St Andrew, Scotland's patron saint. It is thought that he was crucified on a cross of this shape.
Area:	78,772 square kilometres (30,414 square miles)
Major rivers:	River Tay, 193 kilometres (120 miles) River Spey, 172 kilometres (106 miles) River Clyde, 171 kilometres (106 miles) River Tweed, 156 kilometres (97 miles) River Forth, 105 kilometres (65 miles)

Major lochs:	Loch Lomond, 56 sq kilometres (21 square miles)
	Loch Ness, 56 sq kilometres (21 square miles)
	Loch Awe, 38 sq kilometres (14 square miles)
	Loch Maree, 29 sq kilometres (11 square miles)
Highest elevation:	Ben Nevis, 1,344 metres (4,409 feet)
Currency:	Pound sterling. Scottish banks are allowed to print their own notes, so there are four different designs of each note.
Exports:	Food and drink; chemicals; business services; office machinery
Literacy rates:	99 per cent of the population can read and write
Inventions:	The modified steam engine, waterproof raincoats, tarmacadam (tarmac), penicillin, telephones, and television
Public holidays:	New Year (1 and 2 January), Good Friday, May Day Bank Holiday, Spring Bank Holiday (last Monday in May), Summer Bank Holiday (first Monday in August), St Andrew's day (30 November), Christmas Day (25 December), Boxing Day (26 December).

Timeline

AD is short for *Anno Domini*, which is Latin for "in the year of our Lord".
AD is added before a date and means that the date occurred after the birth of Jesus Christ, for example, AD 720.

AD 80–84	The Roman General Agricola invades Caledonia (the Roman word for Scotland)
AD 142	The Roman Emperor Antonine builds a defensive wall across the narrowest part of Caledonia, between the rivers Clyde and Forth
AD 170	The Romans retreat back to Hadrian's Wall, in northern England, and make no further advances in Caledonia
AD 500s	Scotii (Irish Celts) invade Scotland's west coast. Anglo-Saxons begin settling in the southeastern part of Scotland.
AD 563	Christianity comes to Scotland as St Columba, a missionary from Ireland, founds a religious community on the island of Iona
AD 700s	Vikings invade
AD 843	Kenneth MacAlpin becomes first King of Scotland
1018	King Malcom II defeats Anglo-Saxons and Scotland is born
1232–1469	Vikings give land back to Scotland
1296	King Edward I of England invades Scotland
1297	William Wallace leads Scotland to victory at Stirling Bridge. King Edward I is defeated.
1305	William Wallace is captured and killed
1314	Robert the Bruce leads Scotland to victory at Bannockburn. King Edward II is defeated.
1500s	The Scottish Reformation shakes religion. The Scottish Church begins a country-wide free education system.
1507	The first printing press arrives in Edinburgh
1560	John Knox founds the Presbyterian Protestant religion
1568	The Catholic Mary, Queen of Scots, flees Scotland and her baby son, James VI, is raised as a Protestant
1603	King James VI of Scotland also becomes King James I of England, after Elizabeth I of England dies

1660	Charles II is restored as King of England (and Wales), Scotland, and Ireland
1685	Charles II dies, his brother becomes James VII of Scotland (James II of England)
1688	The Protestant Dutch Prince William of Orange overthrows King James
1707	The Treaty of Union is signed and Scotland ceases to be an independent nation. The United Kingdom is created.
1715	The first Jacobite Uprising. Supporters of the old King James want his son, James Edward, to be restored as King. The rebellion fails.
1745	James Edward's son, Charles Edward Stuart (Bonnie Prince Charlie) leads the second Jacobite Uprising
1746	Bonnie Prince Charlie is defeated at Culloden, near Inverness
1700s 1800s	Highland Clearances force many Scots to emigrate. The Industrial Revolution brings huge advances. Many Irish immigrants arrive.
1801	Scotland's population is 1,608,420
1846	A railway line connects Edinburgh and London
1890	The Forth Railway Bridge is completed
1911	Scotland's population is 4,760,904
1914–1918	World War I. Scotland loses around 100,000 soldiers in the fighting.
1931	Scotland's population begins to decline as people migrate to find better jobs
1939–1945	World War II. Areas in Glasgow, Edinburgh, Aberdeen, and Dundee are bombed.
1900s	Immigrants arrive from Italy, Bangladesh, India, and Pakistan
1947	The first Edinburgh Festival is held
1950s	Large scale conifer planting begins
1976	Large scale oil production in the North Sea begins
1996	Dolly the sheep, the first living mammal to be cloned, is born
1997	A huge majority of Scots vote "yes" in a referendum on devolution and the creation of a Scottish Parliament
May 1999	Elections take place for the new Scottish Parliament
July 1999	The Scottish Parliament is officially opened by Queen Elizabeth II
2000s	Immigrants arrive from Eastern Europe
2003	Dolly the sheep dies
2004	The new Parliament building at Holyrood in Edinburgh is officially opened
2005	**G8** Summit takes place in Gleneagles Hotel, near Perth, where world leaders meet to discuss global challenges

Glossary

Anglo-Saxon people, originally from Germany, who lived in England before the Norman Conquest in 1066

bagpipes wind instrument made of a leather bag and pipes

ballad poems or songs that tell stories

Catholic branch of Christianity which is led by the Pope

Celtic to do with the Celts, an ancient group of tribes that lived in Scotland, Ireland, Wales, and parts of Cornwall and northern France

clone create an identical copy using complex scientific methods

culture practices, traditions, and beliefs of a society

curling game played on ice in which two teams slide a stone towards a circle at either end

deer stalking tracking and hunting deer to shoot

economy to do with money and the industry and jobs in a country

ecosystem community of living things

emigrate leave one country to live in another

endangered in danger of extinction

erosion wearing away of the earth's surface by wind, water or ice

esplanade level, open expanse of pavement

extinction dying out of a species

famine large-scale lack of food over a wide area

fault crack in the rock that makes up the earth's crust

G8 group of the eight richest countries in the world

haggis dish made of sheep or calf organs that are minced, then mixed with suet, oatmeal, and seasonings

heathland open areas of remote land

Highland region or area of a country which has many hills or mountains

immigrant people who move to live in another country from their native land

import buy goods from another country

industrialized affected by many different kinds of industry

Industrial Revolution changes that took place in how goods were made, from small scale production by people to large factories in which machines did most of the work. The Industrial Revolution began in the late 1700s in England.

investor person or company who puts money into a business

manufacturing making things in large quantities using machines

migrate change habitat or location, usually when the seasons change

moorland areas of high land that are covered in low-lying vegetation

noble person of high rank or title

parliament group of people who make the laws for a country

peat bogland wet areas with soil that is made up of decayed plants. Peat can be used as a fuel or fertilizer.

plantation large area of land where one type of plant is grown to sell

poet laureate poet honoured by royalty and expected to write poems for celebratory occasions and of national significance

policy rule or plan that is used as a guide for action

population density number of people living in a certain area

primeval prehistoric or primitive

Protestant branch of Christianity which is separate from the Catholic or Orthodox church

renewable energy natural source of energy that will never run out, such as solar or wind energy

species type of animal, bird, or fish

suet hard fat from around the kidneys or loins of cattle or sheep

tartan woollen cloth woven into a plaid design

tax money paid by people to the government. Taxes can come from wages or be placed on goods that people buy.

tenant people who occupy or use another's house, building, office, or land, usually in exchange for rent

textile cloth or fabric

thistle plant with prickly leaves and a head of purple flowers

topography natural and artificial physical features of an area

tribe independent social group, historically often made up of primitive or nomadic people

unemployment percentage of workers that do not have jobs

uninhabited not lived in

urban having to do with a city or a town

vote to choose. People vote for someone to win an election.

Find out more

Books

DK Eyewitness Travel Guide: Scotland, Juliet Clough et al (Dorling Kindersley, 2008)

Horrible Histories: Scotland, Terry Deary (Scholastic, 2009)

Step-Up Geography: Scotland, Alan Rodgers and Angella Streluk (Evans Brothers, 2006)

Stories from Scotland, Barbara Ker Wilson (Oxford University Press, 2009)

Websites

www.visitscotland.com
Visit the official website of Scotland's national tourism organization. Find out what to do and where to do it. Find accommodation and places to eat. If you want to travel in an eco-friendly way, there is a section on green tourism.

www.visitscotland.org
Look at the business website of Scotland's national tourism organization for statistics and information on Scotland's tourism industry.

www.gro-scotland.gov.uk
Visit the website of the General Register Office for Scotland to look at Census data and Scottish family history records.

www.activity-scotland.org.uk
The Activity Scotland Association is an organization that represents providers of activities throughout Scotland. All activity organizations listed on their website must meet strict safety and quality levels. Activities listed range from sea kayaking to pony trekking to fishing.

www.ltscotland.org.uk
Learning and Teaching Scotland is an organization funded by the Scottish Government to transform education in Scotland. The "Scotland's History" section on its website contains a wealth of information and images about Scotland through the ages.

Places to visit

If you ever get the chance to explore Scotland, these organizations can help you plan your visit:

Historic Scotland

This organization is responsible for safeguarding Scotland's historic environment, and encourages people to understand and enjoy it. It cares for 345 historic sites, from wreck sites to ruined castles to ancient wells.

The National Trust for Scotland

This charity works to protect and promote the natural and cultural heritage of Scotland. It owns St Kilda, a World Heritage Site, 16 islands, 7 national nature reserves, 26 castles, palaces, and country houses, 4 battle sites and 35 gardens. Its motto is "A place for everyone".

Scottish Natural Heritage

This organization's job is to encourage people to care for and improve the natural heritage of Scotland. It teaches people how to understand Scottish heritage and enjoy it responsibly. Its motto is "All of nature for all of Scotland".

Topic tools

You can use these topic tools for your school projects. Trace the map onto a sheet of paper, using the thick black outline to guide you.

The Scottish flag is known as the Saltire. There is a legend that the Scottish King Angus looked up at the blue sky during a battle and saw a white saltire (diagonal cross), and this was the origin of the flag. The flag is also known as St Andrew's Cross, after St Andrew, the patron saint of Scotland. Copy the flag design and then colour in your picture. Make sure you use the right colours!

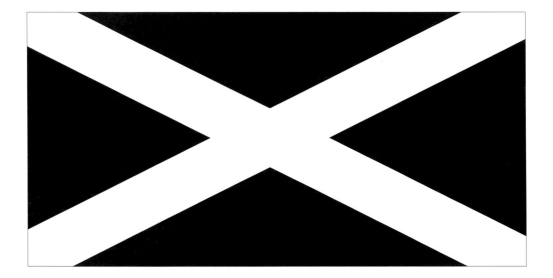

N

Edinburgh

Index